WELCOME TO THE KINGDOM WORKBOOK

A GUIDE FOR DEEPER KINGDOM LIVING

CHARLES E. MEUX, JR.

Largo, MD

Copyright © 2025 by Charles E. Meux, Jr.

All rights reserved under the international copyright law. No part of this book may be reproduced or transmitted in any form or by any means, electronic or mechanical, including photocopying, recording, or by any information storage and retrieval system, without the express written permission of the publisher or the author. The exception is reviewers, who may quote brief passages in a review.

Christian Living Books, Inc.
christianlivingbooks.com
We bring your dreams to fruition.

ISBN 9781562296506

All Scripture quotations are taken from the New King James Version®, copyright © 1982 by Thomas Nelson. Used by permission. All rights reserved.

TABLE OF CONTENTS

Introduction 1

Kingdom Self-Reflection Guide: Deepening Your Journey 2

Chapter 1: What Is the Kingdom of God? 6

Chapter 2: Developing Your Character Through Christ 9

Chapter 3: Understanding God's Salvation 13

Chapter 4: New Creation in Christ Jesus 17

Chapter 5: Eternal Life 21

Chapter 6: Baptism: Take the First Step 24

Chapter 7: The Remnant Church 28

Chapter 8: The Bible 32

Chapter 9: Scripture Memory and Meditation 36

Chapter 10: Lord, Teach Us to Pray 40

Chapter 11: Kingdom Stewardship 44

Chapter 12: The Power of Kingdom Community 48

Final Reflection: Royal Progress 52

INTRODUCTION

Your journey into deeper Kingdom living begins now! Your choice to engage with this workbook shows your hunger to move beyond surface understanding to genuine transformation. I believe God has divinely orchestrated this moment in your spiritual journey.

When I wrote *Welcome to the Kingdom*, I envisioned more than sharing information—I wanted to spark a revolution in how believers experience God's Kingdom reality in their daily lives. This workbook is designed to help you activate each Kingdom principle, turning revelation into application. Scripture reminds us that we must "be doers of the word, and not hearers only" (James 1:22). True transformation happens when we apply what we learn. This workbook bridges the gap between knowledge and practice, helping you implement Kingdom truths in every area of your life.

Think of the main book as planting seeds of Kingdom truth, and this workbook as the process of cultivating those seeds until they produce abundant fruit in your life. Each exercise, reflection question, and declaration is designed to help Kingdom principles take root in your heart and manifest in your daily experience.

To gain the most from this workbook:

- Set aside uninterrupted time to thoughtfully engage with each section
- Use a dedicated journal to expound on reflections and for certain exercises
- Be completely honest in your responses—this journey is between you and God
- Personalize the declarations to reflect your unique relationship with God
- Consider working through this material with a trusted friend or small group
- Revisit the Kingdom Self-Reflection section to celebrate your growth

I believe God has something extraordinary for you in these pages. There may be moments when certain exercises challenge you or when implementing specific principles feels difficult. During those times, remember that transformation is a process. Be patient with yourself, rely on the Holy Spirit, and keep pressing forward. Even small steps of obedience move you deeper into Kingdom reality.

As you begin this journey, know that I'm praying for you. I'm asking God to open the eyes of your understanding, to strengthen you with His power in your inner being, and to empower you to live as a vibrant ambassador of His Kingdom on Earth.

In His Service,
Pastor Charles E. Meux, Jr.

KINGDOM SELF-REFLECTION GUIDE: DEEPENING YOUR JOURNEY

This guide uses the KINGDOM framework to help you assess seven critical dimensions of your Kingdom citizenship, providing a comprehensive baseline against which you can measure your growth throughout this workbook journey. For each dimension below, honestly assess where you are on a scale of 1-10 (1 being very weak, 10 being very strong). Then, write brief reflections on your current reality and desired growth in each area. Return to this assessment after completing the workbook to measure your progress.

K - KNOWLEDGE OF KINGDOM PRINCIPLES | Current Rating (1-10): _____

1. What is your current understanding of God's Kingdom? How familiar are you with Kingdom principles taught in Scripture? _____

_____

_____

_____

2. What specific aspects of Kingdom knowledge do you want to develop through this workbook?

_____

_____

_____

_____

I - IDENTITY AS A KINGDOM CITIZEN | Current Rating (1-10): _____

1. How consistently do you live from your identity as a citizen of God's Kingdom rather than from your natural identity? _____

_____

_____

2. What aspects of your Kingdom identity do you most need to strengthen or embrace?

_____

_____

_____

N - NOBLE CHARACTER DEVELOPMENT | Current Rating (1-10): _____

1. How well does your character currently reflect Kingdom values rather than worldly values?

_____

_____

_____

2. What specific character qualities do you want to develop as you grow in Kingdom citizenship?

_____

_____

_____

G - GRACE MANIFESTATION | Current Rating (1-10): _____

1. How readily do you receive God's grace for yourself and extend it to others?

_____

_____

_____

2. In what relationships or situations do you need to experience or express more of God's grace?

_____

_____

D - DOMINION AND AUTHORITY | Current Rating (1-10): _____

1. How confidently do you exercise the spiritual authority Christ has given you?

   _____

   _____

2. In what areas do you need to grow in exercising Kingdom authority and dominion?

   _____

   _____

   _____

O - OBEDIENCE AND ALIGNMENT | Current Rating (1-10): _____

1. How consistently do your decisions align with Kingdom principles rather than worldly wisdom?

   _____

   _____

   _____

2. In what specific areas of life do you need greater obedience and alignment with God's ways?

   _____

   _____

   _____

M - MISSION FULFILLMENT | Current Rating (1-10): _____

1. How actively are you participating in advancing God's Kingdom purposes through your unique gifts and calling? _____

   _____

   _____

2. What aspects of your Kingdom purpose or mission need greater clarity or activation?

SUMMARY REFLECTION

1. Based on your ratings above, what are your strongest areas as a Kingdom citizen?

2. Based on your ratings above, what are your most significant growth opportunities?

3. What are the top 3 outcomes you hope to achieve through completing this workbook?

   a)

   b)

   c)

Remember: This self-assessment is not about performance or comparison but about honest reflection that positions you for greater growth. The Holy Spirit is your ultimate guide in this process of transformation.

He who has begun a good work in you will complete it until the day of Jesus Christ. (Philippians 1:6)

Notes:

Chapter 1:
WHAT IS THE KINGDOM OF GOD?

The Kingdom of God represents far more than a future hope or religious concept—it is the dynamic rule and reign of God manifesting in our lives today. In this chapter, we explore the foundational understanding of God's Kingdom as the lens through which we perceive His plans and the power by which Heaven's reality invades Earth. Understanding God's Kingdom principles transforms how we view ourselves, others, and every circumstance we encounter.

SOUL SEARCHING

1. In your own words, how would you define the Kingdom of God? How is this different from how you understood it before reading this chapter? _____
   _____
   _____
   _____

2. What does it mean that the Kingdom is "not a distant hope but a present reality"? Give an example of how you've seen (or would like to see) Heaven's reality invade Earth.
   _____
   _____
   _____
   _____

3. How does being a citizen of God's Kingdom impact your daily life and decision-making?
   _____
   _____

MEMORIZE & MEDITATE

"But seek first the kingdom of God and His righteousness, and all these things shall be added to you."

(Matthew 6:33)

KINGDOM ACTIVATION

1. **Kingdom Culture Contrast** – List 3 ways your current habits and behaviors align with Kingdom culture. Then identify 3 areas where you need to adjust to better reflect Kingdom values.

   Kingdom Alignment   **Areas for Growth**

   _____   _____

   _____   _____

   _____   _____

2. **Kingdom Authority Activation** – In your journal, write about a specific situation in your life where you need to see Heaven's authority manifested. What would it look like for God's Kingdom to come in this situation?

3. **Kingdom Practices Implementation** – Choose one Kingdom practice mentioned in the chapter (worship, prayer, Word study, etc.) and create a specific plan to strengthen this practice in your daily life over the next week.

   Practice: _____

   _____

   My plan to implement this:

   Day 1: _____

   _____

   Day 2: _____

   _____

   Day 3: _____

   _____

Day 4: _____
_____

Day 5: _____
_____

Day 6: _____
_____

Day 7: _____
_____

KINGDOM TERRITORY EXPANSION

1. **Territory to Claim**: In your journal, identify one specific area of your life that needs to come under Kingdom rule and authority.
2. **Royal Proclamation**: Write a declaration based on this chapter's Kingdom principles that claims this territory for God's Kingdom. Speak this over the situation daily.
3. **Occupation Strategy**: What specific actions will you take this week to establish Kingdom reality in this area:
4. **Resistance Assessment**: What opposing forces might you encounter, and what biblical strategies will you use to overcome them?
5. **Advancement Timeline**: When will you begin each action step? Who will you share this with for accountability and support in claiming this territory?

ROYAL DECLARATION

I am being transformed by the revelation of God's Kingdom. My mind is renewed to think from Heaven's perspective, not Earth's. I see myself as God sees me. I am a citizen of Heaven stationed on Earth with divine authority. The same power that raised Christ from the dead lives in me. I represent the Kingdom well in every area of my life, and I manifest Heaven's reality wherever I go.

Notes: _____
_____
_____

Chapter 2:
Developing Your Character Through Christ

Character development lies at the heart of our spiritual journey. As we surrender to Christ's transformative work, we increasingly reflect His nature to the world around us. This chapter explores how the Holy Spirit shapes our character, producing the fruit that authenticates our identity as Kingdom citizens. Through intentional cooperation with God's refining process, we become living testimonies of Christ's character in a world desperately needing authentic examples of godliness.

SOUL SEARCHING

1. What areas of Christ's character do you most want to develop in your own life, and why do these particular traits matter to you? _____

_____

_____

_____

_____

2. Which of the fruit of the Spirit currently flourishes most evidently in your life, and which one needs the most cultivation? _____

_____

_____

_____

_____

3. How have you experienced being "transformed from glory to glory" in a specific area of your life?

_____
_____
_____
_____
_____

MEMORIZE & MEDITATE

"I have been crucified with Christ; it is no longer I who live, but Christ lives in me; and the life which I now live in the flesh I live by faith in the Son of God, who loved me and gave Himself for me."

(Galatians 2:20)

KINGDOM ACTIVATION

1. **Fruit Assessment** – Honestly evaluate yourself on each fruit of the Spirit on a scale of 1-10 (1 being very weak, 10 being very strong). For each quality, write one specific way you could strengthen it in your daily life.

Fruit	Rating (1-10)	Plan to Strengthen
Love	_____	_____
Joy	_____	_____
Peace	_____	_____
Patience	_____	_____
Kindness	_____	_____
Goodness	_____	_____
Faithfulness	_____	_____
Gentleness	_____	_____
Self-control	_____	_____

2. **Glory to Glory Timeline** – Identify one character trait that has changed in you since becoming a believer. Write about how this transformation occurred and what role the Holy Spirit played in the process.

_____

_____

_____

_____

_____

_____

_____

_____

_____

_____

3. **Christ-like Response** – Think of a challenging relationship or situation you're currently facing. How would Jesus respond in this situation? What character traits would He display?

_____

_____

_____

_____

_____

_____

_____

_____

_____

KINGDOM TERRITORY EXPANSION

1. **Territory to Claim**: In your journal, identify one specific character trait that needs to come under Christ's lordship and transformation.
2. **Royal Proclamation**: Write a declaration based on Christ's character and your identity in Him that claims this aspect of your character for God's Kingdom.
3. **Occupation Strategy**: List specific actions you will take this week to establish Christ's nature in this area.
4. **Resistance Assessment**: What opposing forces might you encounter, and what biblical strategies will you use to overcome them?
5. **Advancement Timeline**: When will you begin each action step? Who will you share this with for accountability and support in claiming this territory?

ROYAL DECLARATION

I am being transformed into the image of Christ through the renewing of my mind. His nature is my nature. His character is my character. Pride has no place in me because I embrace the humility of Christ. My heart overflows with jubilation, praise, and gratitude to my Lord and Savior. I rest in the reality that He lives in me, and His life flows through me.

Notes:

CHAPTER 3:

UNDERSTANDING GOD'S SALVATION

Salvation forms the very foundation of our Christian faith, yet its depths and implications often exceed our initial understanding. This chapter explores the multidimensional nature of salvation—past, present, and future—and how it transforms every aspect of our lives. As we grasp the fullness of what Christ accomplished through His finished work, we discover the freedom to live from victory rather than for victory.

SOUL SEARCHING

1. How has your understanding of salvation expanded beyond simply "going to Heaven when you die"?

    _____
    _____
    _____
    _____
    _____

2. How does knowing that salvation includes justification, sanctification, and glorification change how you view your Christian journey? _____
    _____
    _____
    _____
    _____
    _____

3. What does it mean to you that salvation is a gift that cannot be earned, and how does this truth impact your relationship with God? _____

_____

_____

_____

_____

MEMORIZE & MEDITATE

"For by grace you have been saved through faith, and that not of yourselves; it is the gift of God, not of works, lest anyone should boast." (Ephesians 2:8-9)

KINGDOM ACTIVATION

1. **Salvation Mapping** – Create a timeline of your salvation journey, marking significant moments of encountering God's grace and experiencing different aspects of salvation.

_____

_____

_____

_____

_____

_____

_____

_____

2. **Three Dimensions Exploration** – For each dimension of salvation, write about how you've experienced it in your life:

   Justification: How has knowing you're forgiven and declared righteous changed you?

   _____
   _____
   _____
   _____
   _____

   Sanctification: What areas of your life is God currently working on? How are you cooperating with this process?

   _____
   _____
   _____
   _____
   _____
   _____
   _____

   Glorification: How does the hope of future glory impact how you view current struggles?

   _____
   _____
   _____
   _____
   _____
   _____

3. **Grace Response Plan** – List 5 specific ways you can respond to God's gift of salvation this week:

_____
_____
_____
_____

KINGDOM TERRITORY EXPANSION

1. **Territory to Claim**: In your journal, identify one specific area where you need to experience the transformative power of salvation in a deeper way.
2. **Royal Proclamation**: Write a declaration based on your salvation in Christ that claims this area for God's Kingdom.
3. **Occupation Strategy**: List specific actions you will take this week to establish the reality of your salvation in this area:
4. **Resistance Assessment**: What opposing forces might you encounter, and what biblical strategies will you use to overcome them?
5. **Advancement Timeline**: When will you begin each action step? Who will you share this with for accountability and support in claiming this territory?

ROYAL DECLARATION

I stand firmly in the finished work of Christ. The blood of Jesus has cleansed me completely. I am saved, sanctified, and filled with the Holy Spirit. I am righteous in Christ—not by my own works but by His grace. I live from victory, not for victory. What Jesus accomplished at the cross is complete in me. I am forgiven, redeemed, and made whole by the power of the cross.

Notes: _____
_____
_____
_____
_____

Chapter 4:
NEW CREATION IN CHRIST JESUS

Being made a "new creation" in Christ represents one of the most profound transformations possible in human experience. Far more than self-improvement or religious commitment, this divine miracle fundamentally changes our spiritual DNA. This chapter examines what it means to be made new in Christ, exploring how this spiritual reality manifests in our identity, purpose, and daily experience as Kingdom citizens.

SOUL SEARCHING

1. What aspects of your "old self" have been most difficult to leave behind, and how is your new identity in Christ giving you power to overcome? _____

   _____

   _____

   _____

   _____

2. How would you explain the concept of being "born again" to someone who is unfamiliar with Christian terminology? _____

   _____

   _____

   _____

   _____

   _____

3. How does the truth that the Father sees you "as if you never sinned" affect your view of yourself and your approach to failures? _____

_____

_____

_____

_____

MEMORIZE & MEDITATE

"Therefore, if anyone is in Christ, he is a new creation; old things have passed away; behold, all things have become new." (2 Corinthians 5:17)

KINGDOM ACTIVATION

1. **Identity Transformation Chart** Create two columns. In the left column, list aspects of your old identity before Christ. In the right column, write the corresponding truth about your new identity in Christ.

Old Identity	New Identity in Christ

2. **Renewal Zones** – Identify three areas where you need to more fully embrace your new creation reality. These could be thought patterns, habits, relationships, or behaviors. For each area, write a strategy that aligns with your new identity in Christ.

3. **New Birth Narrative** – Write about your born-again experience. If you haven't been born again, write about your thoughts and questions regarding spiritual rebirth. If you can't pinpoint a specific moment, reflect on how you've experienced gradual renewal in Christ.

KINGDOM TERRITORY EXPANSION

1. **Territory to Claim**: In your journal, identify one specific area where you still live according to your old identity rather than your new creation reality.
2. **Royal Proclamation**: Write a declaration based on your new identity in Christ that claims this area for God's Kingdom.
3. **Occupation Strategy**: List specific actions you will take this week to establish your new creation identity in this area:
4. **Resistance Assessment**: What opposing forces might you encounter, and what biblical strategies will you use to overcome them?
5. **Advancement Timeline**: When will you begin each action step? Who will you share this with for accountability and support in claiming this territory?

ROYAL DECLARATION

I am a new creation in Christ. The old has gone; the new has come. What Christ did on the cross removed every burden of self-effort and striving. I have been born again by the incorruptible seed of God's Word. I carry the DNA of Heaven within me. God sees me as if I had never sinned. I live from my new identity, not my old one. Christ's finished work is complete in me, and I walk in the fullness of who He has made me to be.

Notes:

Chapter 5:

ETERNAL LIFE

Eternal life encompasses far more than just unending existence—it represents a divine quality of life that begins the moment we receive Christ. This chapter explores the multi-dimensional nature of God's unstoppable, unquenchable life that now flows within every believer. As we learn to access and operate in this supernatural life, we experience victory over death, sickness, fear, and limitation, manifesting Kingdom reality here and now.

SOUL SEARCHING

1. How has your understanding of eternal life shifted from a future promise to a present reality that impacts your daily existence? _____
_____
_____
_____

2. In what specific areas of your life have you experienced the "unstoppable" or "unquenchable" life of Christ at work? _____
_____
_____
_____

3. How does John 10:10 illuminate the contrast between the enemy's purpose and Christ's purpose in your personal experience? _____
_____
_____
_____

MEMORIZE & MEDITATE

"And this is the testimony: that God has given us eternal life, and this life is in His Son. He who has the Son has life; he who does not have the Son of God does not have life." (1 John 5:11-12)

KINGDOM ACTIVATION

1. **Eternal Life Manifestation** – List specific ways you can see eternal life operating in different areas of your life now:

    In your thoughts: _____

    _____

    In your emotions: _____

    _____

    In your physical health: _____

    _____

    In your relationships: _____

    _____

    In your spiritual growth: _____

    _____

    In your purpose/calling: _____

    _____

2. **Abundance Amplifier** – On a scale of 1-10, rate how much you're experiencing the abundant life Jesus promised in each area below. Then write one specific change you could make to increase that rating.

Life Area	Rating (1-10)	Step to Increase Abundance
Spiritual	_____	_____
Mental	_____	_____
Emotional	_____	_____

Life Area	Rating (1-10)	Step to Increase Abundance
Physical	_____	_____
Relational	_____	_____
Financial	_____	_____
Purpose	_____	_____

3. **Thief Resistance Strategy** – Identify an area where the enemy has been attempting to steal, kill, or destroy in your life. Based on Scripture, how does the eternal life of Christ counter this attack.

_____
_____
_____
_____

KINGDOM TERRITORY EXPANSION

1. **Territory to Claim**: In your journal, identify one specific area where you need God's abundant, eternal life to transform current limitations or death.
2. **Royal Proclamation**: Write a declaration based on the unstoppable nature of God's life in you that claims this area for God's Kingdom.
3. **Occupation Strategy**: List specific actions you will take this week to establish and release eternal life in this area: a. b. c.
4. **Resistance Assessment**: What opposing forces might you encounter, and what biblical strategies will you use to overcome them?
5. **Advancement Timeline**: When will you begin each action step? Who will you share this with for accountability and support in claiming this territory?

ROYAL DECLARATION

I am a carrier of God's unstoppable, unquenchable life. The same Spirit that raised Christ from the dead lives in me. The abundant life Jesus promised is my present reality, not just my future hope. I will not be diminished by the enemy's tactics. In God, I live, move, and have my being. I am positioned for triumph and prosperity in every dimension of life. As a citizen of Heaven, I manifest eternal life in my mortal body. Victory is my inheritance.

Chapter 6:
BAPTISM: TAKE THE FIRST STEP

Water baptism represents a profound act of identification with Christ's death, burial, and resurrection. This chapter explores the biblical significance of baptism and why Jesus commanded all believers to participate in this sacred ordinance as an essential step in their Kingdom journey.

SOUL SEARCHING

1. How would you explain the significance of water baptism to someone who views it as merely a religious ritual? _____

_____

_____

_____

_____

_____

_____

2. What does baptism as identification with Christ's death, burial, and resurrection mean to you personally? _____

_____

_____

_____

_____

_____

_____

3. How does public declaration of faith through baptism strengthen one's walk with Christ?

MEMORIZE & MEDITATE

"Therefore we were buried with Him through baptism into death, that just as Christ was raised from the dead by the glory of the Father, even so we also should walk in newness of life." (Romans 6:4)

KINGDOM ACTIVATION

1. **Baptism Reflection** – Check which statement best applies to you:

    ☐ I have been baptized as a believer by immersion

    ☐ I was christened/baptized as an infant

    ☐ I have never been baptized

    ☐ I am considering baptism

    If you have been baptized as a believer, write about your experience and what it meant to you.

If you haven't been baptized as a believer by immersion, what questions or hesitations do you have?

_____
_____
_____
_____

2. **Faith Declaration Inventory** – In what ways have you publicly declared your faith? If you were to be/ or since being baptized, how would you explain the significance of this step to family and friends who attend? _____

_____
_____
_____
_____
_____
_____

3. **Baptism Action Plan** – If you haven't been baptized and are considering it, what steps do you need to take to prepare for baptism? Who might you talk to about this decision? _____

_____
_____
_____
_____
_____

KINGDOM TERRITORY EXPANSION

1. **Territory to Claim**: In your journal, identify one specific area where you need to experience the reality of being dead to sin and alive to God in Christ.
2. **Royal Proclamation**: Write a declaration based on your baptism identification with Christ that claims this area for God's Kingdom.
3. **Occupation Strategy**: List specific actions you will take this week to establish the power of baptism in this area.
4. **Resistance Assessment**: What opposing forces might you encounter, and what biblical strategies will you use to overcome them?
5. **Advancement Timeline**: When will you begin each action step? Who will you share this with for accountability and support in claiming this territory?

ROYAL DECLARATION

I publicly declare my allegiance to Christ and His Kingdom. I am buried with Christ and raised to walk in newness of life. The waters of baptism have marked me as Christ's own. I have crossed over from death to life, from darkness to light. God's goodness and blessing flow through my life. I am renewed and refreshed daily by the power of the Holy Spirit. My identity is secure in Christ.

Notes:

Chapter 7:
THE REMNANT CHURCH

Throughout history, God has always preserved a faithful remnant—those who remain true to His Word and purposes despite cultural pressures to compromise. This chapter explores what it means to be part of this remnant in our generation, examining the characteristics, calling, and responsibilities of believers who choose to stand firm in their faith while extending God's love to a world in desperate need of authentic Kingdom representation.

SOUL SEARCHING

1. What does it mean to you to be part of the "remnant" of God in this generation, and how does this identity shape your daily choices? _____
_____
_____
_____
_____

2. How does the story of the three Hebrew boys in the fiery furnace inspire you to stand firm in your faith today? _____
_____
_____
_____
_____

3. In what ways have you experienced the tension between Kingdom values and cultural pressures in your own life? _____

_____

_____

_____

_____

MEMORIZE & MEDITATE

"Yet for us there is but one God, the Father, from whom are all things and we exist for Him; and one Lord, Jesus Christ, by whom are all things, and we exist through Him." (1 Corinthians 8:6)

KINGDOM ACTIVATION

1. **Cultural Discernment Matrix** – Identify three specific messages, trends, or values in today's culture that contradict Kingdom principles. For each one, write down the corresponding Kingdom truth and how you can stand firm in that truth.

Cultural Message	Kingdom Truth	How to Stand Firm
_____	_____	_____
_____	_____	_____
_____	_____	_____

2. **Remnant Declarations** – What does it means for you personally to be part of God's remnant in this generation:

   o I am... _____

   o I will... _____

   o I refuse to... _____

- o I choose to... _____
- o I stand for... _____
- o I represent... _____
- o I carry... _____

3. **Fourth Man Testimony** – Describe a "fiery furnace" situation in your life where God showed up as "the fourth man" and delivered you. What did this experience teach you about God's faithfulness and protection?

_____
_____
_____
_____
_____
_____
_____
_____
_____
_____

KINGDOM TERRITORY EXPANSION

1. **Territory to Claim**: In your journal, identify one specific area where you need to firmly establish God's Kingdom standards despite cultural pressure to compromise.
2. **Royal Proclamation**: Write a declaration based on your identity as part of God's remnant that claims this area for God's Kingdom.
3. **Occupation Strategy**: List specific actions you will take this week to establish Kingdom truth in this area.
4. **Resistance Assessment**: What opposing forces might you encounter, and what biblical strategies will you use to overcome them?

5. **Advancement Timeline**: When will you begin each action step? Who will you share this with for accountability and support in claiming this territory?

ROYAL DECLARATION

I am part of God's faithful remnant in this generation. I stand firmly for truth when others compromise. Like the three Hebrew boys, I will not bow to the idols of this age. The fire of opposition reveals the presence of the Fourth Man walking with me. God watches over me and protects me from evil. I declare that Jesus Christ is Lord over every nation and people group. His name will be exalted in the earth.

Notes:

Chapter 8:

THE BIBLE

God's Word stands as our unshakeable foundation, our guide for life, and our source of truth in an ever-changing world. This chapter explores how to approach, understand, and apply Scripture in ways that transform our daily lives and build our faith. The Bible is not merely an ancient religious text but a living, active revelation that speaks into every situation we face, providing divine wisdom and supernatural power for Kingdom living.

SOUL SEARCHING

1. How has your view of the Bible evolved from seeing it as merely a rule book to understanding it as God's living Word? _____
_____
_____
_____
_____
_____

2. What does it mean that the Bible has "one message: the establishment of the Kingdom of God through Christ Jesus"? _____
_____
_____
_____
_____
_____

3. How has Scripture functioned as "a lamp to your feet and a light to your path" in a specific situation in your life? _____

_____

_____

_____

_____

MEMORIZE & MEDITATE

"For the word of God is living and powerful, and sharper than any two-edged sword, piercing even to the division of soul and spirit, and of joints and marrow, and is a discerner of the thoughts and intents of the heart." (Hebrews 4:12)

KINGDOM ACTIVATION

1. **Bible Engagement Evaluation** – Honestly evaluate your current Bible reading habits:

    How often do you read the Bible? _____

    When and where do you typically read? _____

    _____

    What method do you use (devotional, by verse, topical, etc.)? _____

    _____

    What challenges do you face in consistent Bible reading? _____

    _____

    _____

    What changes would help you engage more deeply with Scripture? _____

    _____

    _____

2. **Scripture Immersion Practice** – In your journal, choose a passage mentioned in the chapter that particularly spoke to you. Use the following method to study it more deeply:

   Write out the passage:
   - ♛ What does this passage say about God?
   - ♛ What does this passage say about humanity?
   - ♛ What principles or commands are contained in this passage?
   - ♛ How can I apply this passage to my life today?
   - ♛ My specific action plan based on this passage:

3. **Kingdom Manifestation Plan** – Identify three specific ways you can better establish God's Kingdom in your daily life based on Scripture:

   1. _____

   2. _____

   3. _____

KINGDOM TERRITORY EXPANSION

1. **Territory to Claim**: In your journal, identify one specific area where you need God's Word to transform worldly thinking and establish divine truth.
2. **Royal Proclamation**: Write a declaration based on the power and authority of Scripture that claims this area for God's Kingdom.
3. **Occupation Strategy**: List specific actions you will take this week to establish Scripture's authority in this area.
4. **Resistance Assessment**: What opposing forces might you encounter, and what biblical strategies will you use to overcome them?
5. **Advancement Timeline**: When will you begin each action step? Who will you share this with for accountability and support in claiming this territory?

ROYAL DECLARATION

I have the spirit of wisdom and revelation in the knowledge of God. The eyes of my understanding are enlightened to comprehend the hope of His calling and the greatness of His power toward me. God's Word is alive and active in me, transforming my thinking and reshaping my reality. Scripture is my foundation, my weapon, and my guide. I build my life on the unshakable truth of God's Word.

Notes:

Chapter 9:
SCRIPTURE MEMORY AND MEDITATION

In a world filled with distractions and competing voices, Scripture memory and meditation provide powerful pathways to spiritual transformation. This chapter explores practical approaches to hiding God's Word in our hearts and meditating on its truths. These disciplines are not religious duties but profound encounters with the living Word that renew our minds, strengthen our faith, and equip us to navigate life's challenges with Heaven's perspective.

SOUL SEARCHING

1. How have you experienced the "living power" of Scripture in your own life when you've internalized passages beyond simple reading? _____
   _____
   _____
   _____
   _____

2. What obstacles have prevented you from developing a consistent Scripture memory practice?
   _____
   _____
   _____
   _____
   _____

3. How does hiding God's Word in your heart serve as spiritual protection and empowerment?

MEMORIZE & MEDITATE

"This Book of the Law shall not depart from your mouth, but you shall meditate in it day and night, that you may observe to do according to all that is written in it. For then you will make your way prosperous, and then you will have good success." (Joshua 1:8)

KINGDOM ACTIVATION

1. **Scripture Selection** – Choose three verses from "Welcome to the Kingdom" that particularly spoke to you. Write them below and create a plan to memorize them over the next week:

   Verse 1:

   Verse 2:

   Verse 3:

My Memory Plan:

Day 1: _____

_____

Day 2: _____

_____

Day 3: _____

_____

Day 4: _____

_____

Day 5: _____

_____

Day 6: _____

_____

Day 7: _____

_____

2. **Meditation Practice** – Select one of the verses above. In your journal, practice the meditation steps outlined in the chapter:

   Write the verse

   - ♛ Pause and Ponder (write specific words or phrases that stand out)
   - ♛ Speak It Out (how does it feel to declare this verse aloud?)
   - ♛ Journal Your Insights (what is God revealing through this verse?)
   - ♛ Make it immersive (how might you pray, sing, or illustrate this verse?)

3. **Transformation Tracking** – After practicing meditation on your selected verse for a few days, reflect on how this practice has impacted:

   Your understanding of the verse: _____

   _____

Your ability to recall the verse: _____

_____

_____

Your application of the verse in daily life: _____

_____

_____

Your connection with God through His Word: _____

_____

_____

KINGDOM TERRITORY EXPANSION

1. **Territory to Claim**: In your journal, identify one specific area where you need the transforming power of God's Word to renew your mind and establish Kingdom thinking.
2. **Royal Proclamation**: Write a declaration based on Scripture that directly addresses this area and claims it for God's Kingdom.
3. **Occupation Strategy**: List specific actions you will take this week to establish God's Word in this area.
4. **Resistance Assessment**: What opposing forces might you encounter, and what biblical strategies will you use to overcome them?
5. **Advancement Timeline**: When will you begin each action step? Who will you share this with for accountability and support in claiming this territory?

ROYAL DECLARATION

The Word of God dwells richly in me. As I meditate day and night, I become like a tree planted by rivers of water—fruitful and prosperous in all I do. My mind is being renewed by the living Word. I hide Scripture in my heart that I might not sin against God. The Holy Spirit breathes revelation on every verse I study. God's Word guides me, anchors me, and draws me deeper into His presence.

Notes: _____

_____

_____

Chapter 10:

LORD, TEACH US TO PRAY

Prayer remains one of the most vital yet often misunderstood aspects of our relationship with God. This chapter explores the model prayer Jesus provided His disciples, offering practical insights into developing a vibrant prayer life that connects us with God's heart and purposes. Beyond religious ritual, prayer is the divine conversation that positions us to experience Heaven's reality on Earth and participate in establishing God's Kingdom in every sphere of influence.

SOUL SEARCHING

1. How does addressing God as "Father" change your approach to prayer compared to viewing Him as a distant deity? _____
_____
_____
_____
_____

2. What would it look like in your life to truly pray "Your Kingdom come, Your will be done on earth as it is in Heaven"? _____
_____
_____
_____
_____

3. How have you experienced the connection between receiving forgiveness and extending it to others?

_____

_____

_____

_____

MEMORIZE & MEDITATE

"And whatever you ask in My name, that I will do, that the Father may be glorified in the Son. If you ask anything in My name, I will do it." (John 14:13-14)

KINGDOM ACTIVATION

1. **Prayer Personalization** –Rewrite each line of the Lord's Prayer in your own words, making it personal and specific to your current life situation:

Our Father in Heaven, hallowed be Your name _____

_____

_____

Your Kingdom come, Your will be done on Earth as it is in Heaven _____

_____

_____

Give us this day our daily bread _____

_____

_____

And forgive us our debts, as we forgive our debtors _____
_____
_____

And do not lead us into temptation, but deliver us from the evil one _____
_____
_____

2. **Freedom Through Forgiveness** – In your journal, make a private list of people you need to forgive. Next to each name, write a brief prayer releasing them to God. If you're struggling to forgive someone, write about what makes forgiveness difficult in this situation and ask God for help.

3. **Kingdom Breakthrough Targets** – Identify 3 specific areas where you need to see God's Kingdom manifest in your life or circumstances. _____
_____
_____

In your journal, create a structured prayer for each area that:

- ♛ Acknowledges God's sovereignty
- ♛ Declares relevant Scripture promises
- ♛ Makes specific requests aligned with God's will
- ♛ Expresses faith and thanksgiving for the answer

KINGDOM TERRITORY EXPANSION

1. **Territory to Claim**: In your journal, identify one specific area where your prayer life needs transformation or where you need to see answered prayer establish God's authority.
2. **Royal Proclamation**: Write a declaration based on what Scripture says about prayer that claims this area for God's Kingdom.

3. **Occupation Strategy**: List specific actions you will take this week to establish prayer authority in this area.
4. **Resistance Assessment**: What opposing forces might you encounter, and what biblical strategies will you use to overcome them?
5. **Advancement Timeline**: When will you begin each action step? Who will you share this with for accountability and support in claiming this territory?

ROYAL DECLARATION

I declare the will of Heaven into the earth. When I pray, mountains move. As I speak God's Word in faith, His Kingdom advances and darkness retreats. I forgive as I have been forgiven, breaking every chain of resentment. I am delivered from all evil because greater is He who is in me than he who is in the world. My prayers are powerful and effective because I pray in alignment with God's heart.

Notes:

CHAPTER 11:

KINGDOM STEWARDSHIP

Stewardship extends far beyond managing money—it encompasses every resource God entrusts to us as citizens of His Kingdom. This chapter examines what it means to be faithful managers of God's provisions, whether material possessions, spiritual gifts, relationships, or opportunities. Through proper stewardship, we position ourselves to fulfill our divine purpose while advancing God's Kingdom on Earth through multiplication and increase.

SOUL SEARCHING

1. How does viewing yourself as a steward rather than an owner change your approach to managing resources? _____

_____

_____

_____

_____

2. Which of the servants in the parable of the talents do you most identify with, and what does this reveal about your stewardship mindset? _____

_____

_____

_____

_____

3. What God-given talents or resources have you hesitated to develop or invest, and what might be holding you back? _____

_____

_____

_____

_____

_____

MEMORIZE & MEDITATE

"Well done, good and faithful servant; you were faithful over a few things, I will make you ruler over many things. Enter into the joy of your lord." (Matthew 25:21)

KINGDOM ACTIVATION

1. **Resource Inventory** – List the specific talents, gifts, abilities, resources, and opportunities God has entrusted to you. For each one, note how you're currently using it for Kingdom purposes and how you might increase its impact:

Talent/Resource	Current Use	Growth Opportunity

2. **Stewardship Scorecard** – Evaluate your stewardship in each of the following areas on a scale of 1-10 (1 being poor stewardship, 10 being excellent stewardship). For each area, identify one specific action you could take to improve:

Area	Rating	Improvement Action
Time	_____	_____
Money	_____	_____
Relationships	_____	_____
Spiritual Gifts	_____	_____
Health	_____	_____
Knowledge/Education	_____	_____
Influence/Platform	_____	_____

3. **Kingdom Enterprise Blueprint** – If you were to start a Kingdom-focused business or ministry initiative, what would it be? In your journal, create a brief outline that includes:

   - The vision/purpose
   - Who it would serve
   - What need it would meet
   - How it would advance God's Kingdom
   - First three steps to bring it to reality

KINGDOM TERRITORY EXPANSION

1. **Territory to Claim**: In your journal, identify one specific area of resources or assets that needs to come under God's lordship and multiplication principles.
2. **Royal Proclamation**: Write a declaration based on biblical stewardship principles that claims this area for God's Kingdom.
3. **Occupation Strategy**: List specific actions you will take this week to establish godly stewardship in this area.
4. **Resistance Assessment**: What opposing forces might you encounter, and what biblical strategies will you use to overcome them?
5. **Advancement Timeline**: When will you begin each action step? Who will you share this with for accountability and support in claiming this territory?

ROYAL DECLARATION

Everything I have comes from God's hand, and I steward it for His Kingdom purposes. I am faithful with what He has entrusted to me—my time, talents, relationships, and resources. I see every economic opportunity through Heaven's perspective. My stewardship multiplies resources for God's glory and extends His influence in the marketplace. I create wealth with purpose and transfer inheritance with Kingdom values. God's abundance flows through me to bless others.

Notes:

Chapter 12:
THE POWER OF KINGDOM COMMUNITY

The Christian faith was never meant to be lived in isolation. From the beginning, God designed us to thrive in authentic community with fellow believers. This chapter explores the vital importance of Kingdom relationships and how they provide the context for spiritual growth, accountability, and expanded Kingdom influence. Through building genuine connections with other believers, we experience the fullness of God's presence and power that transforms both us and the world around us.

SOUL SEARCHING

1. How have you experienced the truth that "the Christian faith was never meant to be lived in isolation"? _____
   _____
   _____
   _____

2. What aspects of the early church community in Acts 2:42 do you find most compelling or challenging? _____
   _____
   _____
   _____

3. What obstacles have you faced in building authentic community with other believers, and how might these be overcome? _____

_____

_____

_____

_____

MEMORIZE & MEDITATE

"And let us consider one another in order to stir up love and good works, not forsaking the assembling of ourselves together, as is the manner of some, but exhorting one another, and so much the more as you see the Day approaching." (Hebrews 10:24-25)

KINGDOM ACTIVATION

1. **Community Connection Checkup** – Evaluate your current level of involvement in a local church community:

   How frequently do you attend church gatherings? _____

   Are you involved in a small group or ministry team? _____

   Do you have accountability relationships with other believers? _____

   How do you contribute your gifts to the body? _____

   _____

   What steps could you take to deepen your involvement? _____

   _____

   _____

   _____

2. **Gifts Discovery Expedition** – Review Romans 12:6-8 and 1 Corinthians 12:7-11. Which gifts do you believe God has given you? _____
   _____
   _____

   How are you currently using these gifts within a community context? _____
   _____
   _____

   If you're not sure about your gifts, who could help you identify and develop them? _____
   _____
   _____

3. **Kingdom Fellowship Roadmap** – Create a practical plan to strengthen your connection to Kingdom community:

   Finding a church home (if needed): _____
   _____
   _____
   _____

   Building closer relationships with fellow believers: _____
   _____
   _____
   _____

   Serving with my gifts and abilities: _____
   _____
   _____
   _____

Participating in corporate prayer and worship: _____

_____

_____

_____

Supporting others in the community: _____

_____

_____

_____

KINGDOM TERRITORY EXPANSION

1. **Territory to Claim**: In your journal, identify one specific area where you need to establish stronger Kingdom community connections and influence.
2. **Royal Proclamation**: Write a declaration based on biblical community principles that claims this area for God's Kingdom.
3. **Occupation Strategy**: List 2-3 specific actions you will take this week to establish godly relationships in this area: a. b. c.
4. **Resistance Assessment**: What opposing forces might you encounter, and what biblical strategies will you use to overcome them?
5. **Advancement Timeline**: When will you begin each action step? Who will you share this with for accountability and support in claiming this territory?

ROYAL DECLARATION

I am connected to the Body of Christ, where my gifts find their purpose and power. The Holy Spirit works through me to strengthen others, and through others to strengthen me. Together, we demonstrate the power of God's Kingdom in ways impossible alone. I overcome every obstacle to authentic community. God is strategically placing me in relationships that advance His purposes and develop His character in me.

FINAL REFLECTION:

ROYAL PROGRESS

Congratulations on completing the *Welcome to the Kingdom Workbook*! Take some time to reflect on your journey through these 12 chapters and create an action plan for continued growth.

1. KINGDOM GROWTH ASSESSMENT

1. Return to the Kingdom Self-Reflection Guide you completed. Compare your initial assessments with where you are now. In which areas have you experienced the most significant growth?

_____

_____

_____

_____

_____

_____

2. Which Kingdom principles have most transformed your thinking and living?

_____

_____

_____

_____

_____

_____

3. How has your understanding of Kingdom citizenship changed through this journey?

BREAKTHROUGH CELEBRATION

1. Identify the most significant breakthrough you experienced while working through this book. How has this changed your daily walk with God?

2. What specific Kingdom declarations or Scriptures have become especially meaningful to you?

3. How have others noticed changes in your life as you've applied these Kingdom principles?

_____
_____
_____
_____
_____

ROYAL COMMITMENT

Based on what you've learned, write a personal commitment statement describing how you intend to live as a Kingdom citizen going forward: _____

_____
_____
_____
_____
_____
_____
_____

KINGDOM ADVANCEMENT STRATEGY

Outline 5 specific, actionable steps you'll take in the next 30 days to continue growing in Kingdom living:

1. _____
_____
_____

2. _____
_____

3. _____

4. _____

5. _____

COVENANT COMPANIONS

List 3 people who can pray with you and hold you accountable to these commitments:

1. _____
2. _____
3. _____

CORONATION PRAYER:

Heavenly Father, I take my place as a royal heir in God's Kingdom. The revelation of Kingdom reality has awakened me to Heaven's perspective. I don't just know about the Kingdom—I carry its presence and power. Every truth revealed becomes a living force in me, transforming my understanding and reshaping my identity. I am a citizen of Heaven, empowered to demonstrate Kingdom realities on Earth. I declare that my life manifests Heaven's culture in every environment I enter. As I seek first the Kingdom, all other things align with God's perfect design. I am positioned strategically by God to extend His influence and bring Heaven's reality to Earth. My sphere of influence becomes a canvas for displaying God's glory. I live from the revelation that I am seated with Christ in heavenly places, and I exercise the authority of that position. Today, I crown Christ as King over every area of my life and embrace my royal assignment as His ambassador on Earth. In Jesus' name. Amen.

Notes:

www.ingramcontent.com/pod-product-compliance
Lightning Source LLC
LaVergne TN
LVHW081400060426
835510LV00016B/1916